My Self Care Checklist

Copyright © Annie Kowalski
All Rights Reserved.
No part of this publication can be used or reproduced in any manner whatsoever without written permission except in the case of brief quotations embodied in critical articles and reviews.
First Edition: 2020

Extra Self Care Challenge For the WEEK

- ❏ Practice mindfulness exercises
- ❏ Watch the sunset
- ❏ Have a bubble bath
- ❏ Do some spring cleaning at home
- ❏ Express gratitude to someone
- ❏ Learn something new
- ❏ Write your thoughts in a journal
- ❏ Eat a healthy snack
- ❏ Achieve a goal
- ❏ Have a glass of wine

Daily Self Care Tracker

Date: _____

Physical Self Care

Emotional & Mental Self Care

Spiritual Self Care

Social Self Care

Thoughts for the day

Tomorrow, I will...

_____

_____

_____

_____

_____

_____

_____

Daily Self Care Tracker

Date: _____

Physical Self Care

Emotional & Mental Self Care

Spiritual Self Care

Social Self Care

Thoughts for the day

Tomorrow, I will...

_____
_____
_____
_____
_____
_____
_____
_____

Daily Self Care Tracker

Date: _____

Physical Self Care

Emotional & Mental Self Care

Spiritual Self Care

Social Self Care

Thoughts for the day

Tomorrow, I will...

_____
_____
_____
_____
_____
_____
_____
_____

Daily Self Care Tracker

Date: _____

Physical Self Care

Emotional & Mental Self Care

Spiritual Self Care

Social Self Care

Thoughts for the day

Tomorrow, I will...

_____
_____
_____
_____
_____
_____
_____
_____

Daily Self Care Tracker

Date: _____

Physical Self Care

Emotional & Mental Self Care

Spiritual Self Care

Social Self Care

Thoughts for the day

Tomorrow, I will...

_____
_____
_____
_____
_____
_____
_____

Daily Self Care Tracker

Date: _____

Physical Self Care

Emotional & Mental Self Care

Spiritual Self Care

Social Self Care

Thoughts for the day

Tomorrow, I will...

_____
_____
_____
_____
_____
_____
_____

Daily Self Care Tracker

Date: _____

Physical Self Care

Emotional & Mental Self Care

Spiritual Self Care

Social Self Care

Thoughts for the day

Tomorrow, I will...

_____
_____
_____
_____
_____
_____
_____

Extra Self Care Challenge For the WEEK

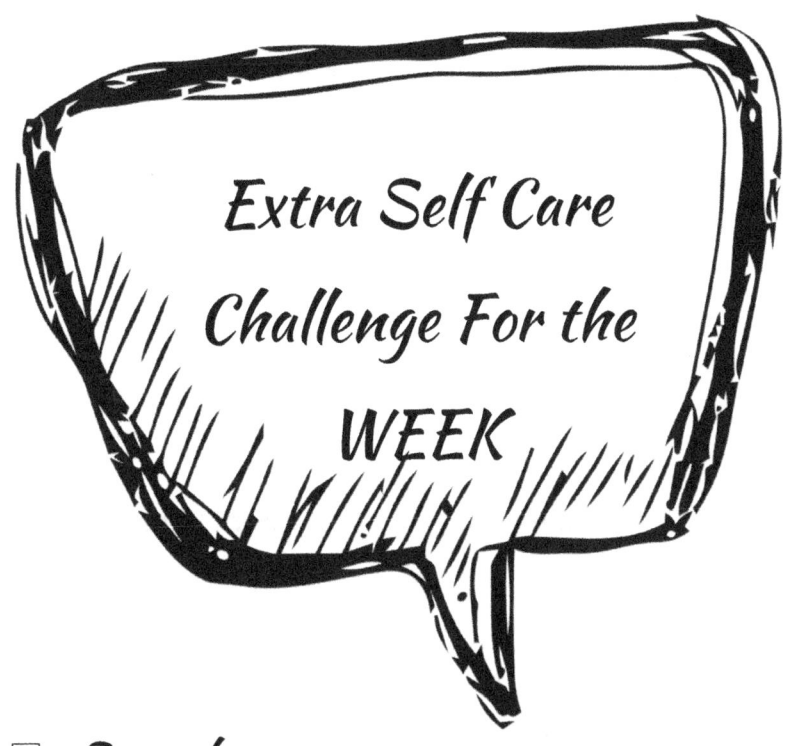

- ❏ Stretch
- ❏ Take a shower
- ❏ Hug someone
- ❏ Pet a dog or cat
- ❏ Discover a new hobby
- ❏ Create a music playlist that makes you happy
- ❏ Go for a walk
- ❏ Take a long bath
- ❏ Read a new book

Daily Self Care Tracker

Date: _____

Physical Self Care

Emotional & Mental Self Care

Spiritual Self Care

Social Self Care

Thoughts for the day

Tomorrow, I will...

_____
_____
_____
_____
_____
_____
_____

Daily Self Care Tracker

Date: _____

Physical Self Care

Emotional & Mental Self Care

Spiritual Self Care

Social Self Care

Thoughts for the day

Tomorrow, I will...

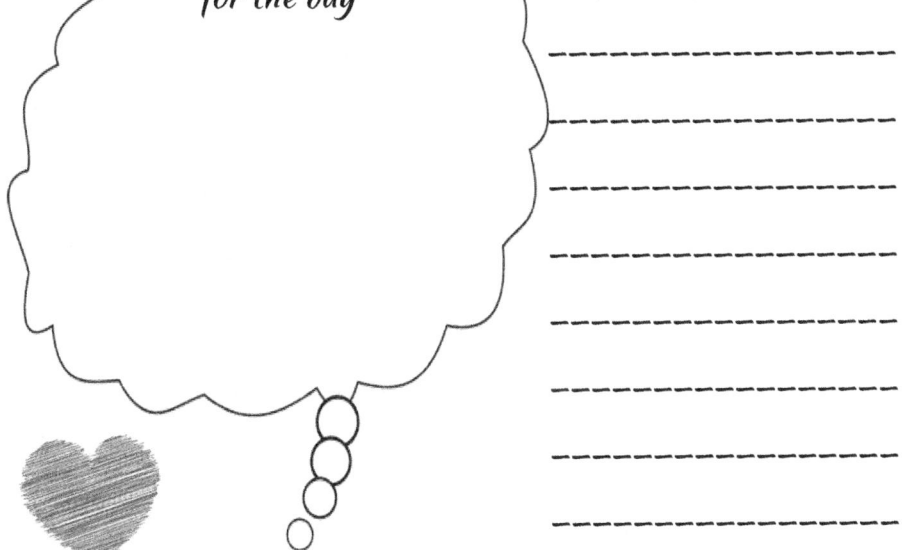

_____
_____
_____
_____
_____
_____
_____

Daily Self Care Tracker

Date: _____

Physical Self Care

Emotional & Mental Self Care

Spiritual Self Care

Social Self Care

Thoughts for the day

Tomorrow, I will...

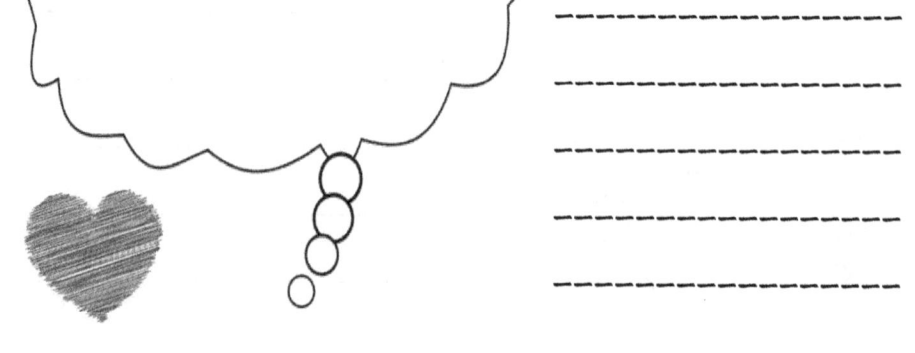

_____
_____
_____
_____
_____
_____
_____
_____

Daily Self Care Tracker

Date: _____

Physical Self Care

Emotional & Mental Self Care

Spiritual Self Care

Social Self Care

Thoughts for the day

Tomorrow, I will...

_____
_____
_____
_____
_____
_____
_____
_____

Daily Self Care Tracker

Date: _____

Physical Self Care

Emotional & Mental Self Care

Spiritual Self Care

Social Self Care

Thoughts for the day

Tomorrow, I will...

_____
_____
_____
_____
_____
_____
_____

Daily Self Care Tracker

Date: _____

Physical Self Care

Emotional & Mental Self Care

Spiritual Self Care

Social Self Care

Thoughts for the day

Tomorrow, I will...

_____
_____
_____
_____
_____
_____
_____

Daily Self Care Tracker

Date: _____

Physical Self Care

Emotional & Mental Self Care

Spiritual Self Care

Social Self Care

Thoughts for the day

Tomorrow, I will...

_____

_____

_____

_____

_____

_____

_____

Extra Self Care Challenge For the WEEK

- ❏ Send a sweet message to a loved one
- ❏ Watch a documentary
- ❏ Eat a healthy meal
- ❏ Try an adult coloring book
- ❏ Say "YES" to something fun
- ❏ Declutter a room or closet at home
- ❏ Take a nap
- ❏ Exercise
- ❏ Spend time outdoors
- ❏ Go for a walk

Daily Self Care Tracker

Date: _____

Physical Self Care

Emotional & Mental Self Care

Spiritual Self Care

Social Self Care

Thoughts for the day

Tomorrow, I will...

_____
_____
_____
_____
_____
_____
_____

Daily Self Care Tracker

Date: _____

Physical Self Care

Emotional & Mental Self Care

Spiritual Self Care

Social Self Care

Thoughts for the day

Tomorrow, I will...

_____
_____
_____
_____
_____
_____
_____
_____

Daily Self Care Tracker

Date: _____

Physical Self Care

Emotional & Mental Self Care

Spiritual Self Care

Social Self Care

Thoughts for the day

Tomorrow, I will...

_____
_____
_____
_____
_____
_____
_____
_____

Daily Self Care Tracker

Date: _____

Physical Self Care

Emotional & Mental Self Care

Spiritual Self Care

Social Self Care

Thoughts for the day

Tomorrow, I will...

_____
_____
_____
_____
_____
_____
_____
_____

Daily Self Care Tracker

Date: _____

Physical Self Care

Emotional & Mental Self Care

Spiritual Self Care

Social Self Care

Thoughts for the day

Tomorrow, I will...

_____
_____
_____
_____
_____
_____
_____

Daily Self Care Tracker

Date: _____

Physical Self Care

Emotional & Mental Self Care

Spiritual Self Care

Social Self Care

Thoughts for the day

Tomorrow, I will...

_____
_____
_____
_____
_____
_____
_____
_____

Daily Self Care Tracker

Date: _____

Physical Self Care

Emotional & Mental Self Care

Spiritual Self Care

Social Self Care

Thoughts for the day

Tomorrow, I will...

_____
_____
_____
_____
_____
_____
_____
_____

Extra Self Care Challenge For the WEEK

- ❏ Unplug for a day
- ❏ Practice a healthy new habit
- ❏ Plan something fun to do today
- ❏ Celebrate a small win
- ❏ Make a feel good playlist and dance to it
- ❏ Fix a home cooked meal
- ❏ Start the day early
- ❏ Watch a funny movie
- ❏ Work on a personal project
- ❏ Meditate

Daily Self Care Tracker

Date: _____

Physical Self Care

Emotional & Mental Self Care

Spiritual Self Care

Social Self Care

Thoughts for the day

Tomorrow, I will...

_____
_____
_____
_____
_____
_____
_____
_____

Daily Self Care Tracker

Date: _____

Physical Self Care

Emotional & Mental Self Care

Spiritual Self Care

Social Self Care

Thoughts for the day

Tomorrow, I will...

_____
_____
_____
_____
_____
_____
_____
_____

Daily Self Care Tracker

Date: _____

Physical Self Care

Emotional & Mental Self Care

Spiritual Self Care

Social Self Care

Thoughts for the day

Tomorrow, I will...

_____
_____
_____
_____
_____
_____
_____

Daily Self Care Tracker

Date: _____

Physical Self Care

Emotional & Mental Self Care

Spiritual Self Care

Social Self Care

Thoughts for the day

Tomorrow, I will...

_____
_____
_____
_____
_____
_____
_____
_____

Daily Self Care Tracker

Date: _____

Physical Self Care

Emotional & Mental Self Care

Spiritual Self Care

Social Self Care

Thoughts for the day

Tomorrow, I will...

_____
_____
_____
_____
_____
_____
_____

Daily Self Care Tracker

Date: _____

Physical Self Care

Emotional & Mental Self Care

Spiritual Self Care

Social Self Care

Thoughts for the day

Tomorrow, I will...

_____
_____
_____
_____
_____
_____
_____
_____

Daily Self Care Tracker

Date: _____

Physical Self Care

Emotional & Mental Self Care

Spiritual Self Care

Social Self Care

Thoughts for the day

Tomorrow, I will...

_____
_____
_____
_____
_____
_____
_____

Extra Self Care Challenge For the WEEK

- ❏ Share your troubles with someone you trust
- ❏ Compliment someone
- ❏ Workout
- ❏ Eat a healthy snack
- ❏ Listen to a podcast
- ❏ Buy something that makes you feel good
- ❏ Explore new TV series
- ❏ Try out a new dinner recipe
- ❏ Make someone smile

Daily Self Care Tracker

Date: _____

Physical Self Care

Emotional & Mental Self Care

Spiritual Self Care

Social Self Care

Thoughts for the day

Tomorrow, I will...

_____
_____
_____
_____
_____
_____
_____

Daily Self Care Tracker

Date: _____

Physical Self Care

Emotional & Mental Self Care

Spiritual Self Care

Social Self Care

Thoughts for the day

Tomorrow, I will...

_____
_____
_____
_____
_____
_____
_____

Daily Self Care Tracker

Date: _____

Physical Self Care

Emotional & Mental Self Care

Spiritual Self Care

Social Self Care

Thoughts for the day

Tomorrow, I will...

_____
_____
_____
_____
_____
_____
_____

Daily Self Care Tracker

Date: _____

Physical Self Care

Emotional & Mental Self Care

Spiritual Self Care

Social Self Care

Thoughts for the day

Tomorrow, I will...

_____
_____
_____
_____
_____
_____
_____
_____

Daily Self Care Tracker

Date: _____

Physical Self Care

Emotional & Mental Self Care

Spiritual Self Care

Social Self Care

Thoughts for the day

Tomorrow, I will...

_____
_____
_____
_____
_____
_____
_____
_____

Daily Self Care Tracker

Date: _____

Physical Self Care

Emotional & Mental Self Care

Spiritual Self Care

Social Self Care

Thoughts for the day

Tomorrow, I will...

_____
_____
_____
_____
_____
_____
_____

Daily Self Care Tracker

Date: _____

Physical Self Care

Emotional & Mental Self Care

Spiritual Self Care

Social Self Care

Thoughts for the day

Tomorrow, I will...

_____
_____
_____
_____
_____
_____
_____

Extra Self Care Challenge For the WEEK

- [ ] Have some "me time"
- [ ] Pamper yourself
- [ ] Drink a glass of water with lemon
- [ ] Connect with family and friends
- [ ] Cook your favorite food
- [ ] Order your favorite takeout
- [ ] Buy an aroma candle
- [ ] Declutter your kitchen or desk
- [ ] Try yoga
- [ ] Take a long bath

Daily Self Care Tracker

Date: _____

Physical Self Care

Emotional & Mental Self Care

Spiritual Self Care

Social Self Care

Thoughts for the day

Tomorrow, I will...

_____
_____
_____
_____
_____
_____
_____
_____

Daily Self Care Tracker

Date: _____

Physical Self Care

Emotional & Mental Self Care

Spiritual Self Care

Social Self Care

Thoughts for the day

Tomorrow, I will...

_____
_____
_____
_____
_____
_____
_____
_____

Daily Self Care Tracker

Date: _____

Physical Self Care

Emotional & Mental Self Care

Spiritual Self Care

Social Self Care

Thoughts for the day

Tomorrow, I will...

_____

_____

_____

_____

_____

_____

Daily Self Care Tracker

Date: _____

Physical Self Care

Emotional & Mental Self Care

Spiritual Self Care

Social Self Care

Thoughts for the day

Tomorrow, I will...

_____
_____
_____
_____
_____
_____
_____
_____

Daily Self Care Tracker

Date: _____

Physical Self Care

Emotional & Mental Self Care

Spiritual Self Care

Social Self Care

Thoughts for the day

Tomorrow, I will...

_____
_____
_____
_____
_____
_____
_____
_____

Daily Self Care Tracker

Date: _____

Physical Self Care

Emotional & Mental Self Care

Spiritual Self Care

Social Self Care

Thoughts for the day

Tomorrow, I will...

_____
_____
_____
_____
_____
_____
_____
_____

Daily Self Care Tracker

Date: _____

Physical Self Care

Emotional & Mental Self Care

Spiritual Self Care

Social Self Care

Thoughts for the day

Tomorrow, I will...

_____
_____
_____
_____
_____
_____
_____

Extra Self Care Challenge For the WEEK

- [ ] Start and work on a personal project
- [ ] Write your thoughts
- [ ] Go for a nature walk
- [ ] Write 3 kind things about yourself
- [ ] Stargaze
- [ ] Buy yourself some flowers
- [ ] Sleep early tonight
- [ ] Do something productive
- [ ] Create a travel bucket list
- [ ] Take a 10-minute break

Daily Self Care Tracker

Date: _____

Physical Self Care

Emotional & Mental Self Care

Spiritual Self Care

Social Self Care

Thoughts for the day

Tomorrow, I will...

_____
_____
_____
_____
_____
_____
_____

Daily Self Care Tracker

Date: _____

Physical Self Care

Emotional & Mental Self Care

Spiritual Self Care

Social Self Care

Thoughts for the day

Tomorrow, I will...

_____
_____
_____
_____
_____
_____
_____

Daily Self Care Tracker

Date: _____

Physical Self Care

Emotional & Mental Self Care

Spiritual Self Care

Social Self Care

Thoughts for the day

Tomorrow, I will...

_____
_____
_____
_____
_____
_____
_____
_____

Daily Self Care Tracker

Date: _____

Physical Self Care

Emotional & Mental Self Care

Spiritual Self Care

Social Self Care

Thoughts for the day

Tomorrow, I will...

_____
_____
_____
_____
_____
_____
_____
_____

Daily Self Care Tracker

Date: _____

Physical Self Care

Emotional & Mental Self Care

Spiritual Self Care

Social Self Care

Thoughts for the day

Tomorrow, I will...

_____
_____
_____
_____
_____
_____
_____

Daily Self Care Tracker

Date: _____

Physical Self Care

Emotional & Mental Self Care

Spiritual Self Care

Social Self Care

Thoughts for the day

Tomorrow, I will...

_____
_____
_____
_____
_____
_____
_____

Daily Self Care Tracker

Date: _____

Physical Self Care

Emotional & Mental Self Care

Spiritual Self Care

Social Self Care

Thoughts for the day

Tomorrow, I will...

_____
_____
_____
_____
_____
_____
_____

Extra Self Care Challenge For the WEEK

- ❏ Take a break from social media
- ❏ Visit your favorite place
- ❏ Enjoy a hearty meal
- ❏ Cook or bake something for your neighbor
- ❏ Meet a friend or family for tea / coffee
- ❏ Take 5 deep breaths
- ❏ Do a home workout
- ❏ Paint your nails
- ❏ Sit in the sun

Daily Self Care Tracker

Date: _____

Physical Self Care

Emotional & Mental Self Care

Spiritual Self Care

Social Self Care

Thoughts for the day

Tomorrow, I will...

_____
_____
_____
_____
_____
_____
_____
_____

Daily Self Care Tracker   Date: _____

Physical Self Care

Emotional & Mental Self Care

Spiritual Self Care

Social Self Care

Thoughts for the day

Tomorrow, I will...

_____
_____
_____
_____
_____
_____
_____
_____

Daily Self Care Tracker

Date: _____

Physical Self Care

Emotional & Mental Self Care

Spiritual Self Care

Social Self Care

Thoughts for the day

Tomorrow, I will...

_____
_____
_____
_____
_____
_____
_____

Daily Self Care Tracker

Date: _____

Physical Self Care

Emotional & Mental Self Care

Spiritual Self Care

Social Self Care

Thoughts for the day

Tomorrow, I will...

_____
_____
_____
_____
_____
_____
_____
_____

Daily Self Care Tracker

Date: _____

Physical Self Care

Emotional & Mental Self Care

Spiritual Self Care

Social Self Care

Thoughts for the day

Tomorrow, I will...

_____
_____
_____
_____
_____
_____
_____
_____

Daily Self Care Tracker

Date: _____

Physical Self Care

Emotional & Mental Self Care

Spiritual Self Care

Social Self Care

Thoughts for the day

Tomorrow, I will...

_____
_____
_____
_____
_____
_____
_____
_____

Daily Self Care Tracker

Date: _____

Physical Self Care

Emotional & Mental Self Care

Spiritual Self Care

Social Self Care

Thoughts for the day

Tomorrow, I will...

_____
_____
_____
_____
_____
_____
_____
_____

Extra Self Care Challenge For the WEEK

- [ ] Say "I Love You" to yourself
- [ ] Treat yourself out for a coffee and a meal
- [ ] Write things you're grateful for
- [ ] Cuddle or play with your pet
- [ ] Meet up with a friend you haven't seen for a long time
- [ ] Try a new salad recipe
- [ ] Find an inspiration
- [ ] Congratulate yourself
- [ ] Run outdoors

Daily Self Care Tracker

Date: _____

Physical Self Care

Emotional & Mental Self Care

Spiritual Self Care

Social Self Care

Thoughts for the day

Tomorrow, I will...

_____
_____
_____
_____
_____
_____
_____

Daily Self Care Tracker

Date: _____

Physical Self Care

Emotional & Mental Self Care

Spiritual Self Care

Social Self Care

Thoughts for the day

Tomorrow, I will...

_____
_____
_____
_____
_____
_____
_____
_____

Daily Self Care Tracker

Date: _____

Physical Self Care

Emotional & Mental Self Care

Spiritual Self Care

Social Self Care

Thoughts for the day

Tomorrow, I will...

_____
_____
_____
_____
_____
_____
_____
_____

Daily Self Care Tracker

Date: _____

Physical Self Care

Emotional & Mental Self Care

Spiritual Self Care

Social Self Care

Thoughts for the day

Tomorrow, I will...

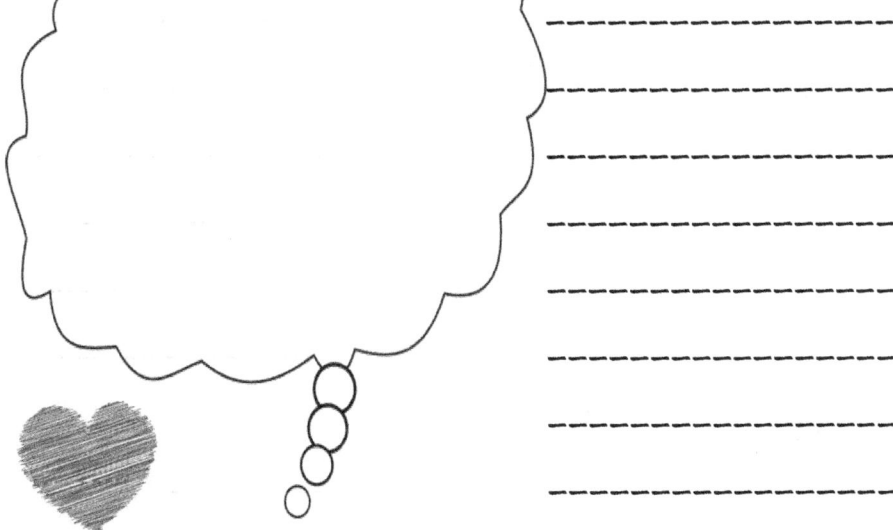

_____
_____
_____
_____
_____
_____
_____
_____

Daily Self Care Tracker

Date: _____

Physical Self Care

Emotional & Mental Self Care

Spiritual Self Care

Social Self Care

Thoughts for the day

Tomorrow, I will...

_____
_____
_____
_____
_____
_____
_____

Daily Self Care Tracker

Date: _____

Physical Self Care

Emotional & Mental Self Care

Spiritual Self Care

Social Self Care

Thoughts for the day

Tomorrow, I will...

_____
_____
_____
_____
_____
_____
_____

Daily Self Care Tracker

Date: _____

Physical Self Care

Emotional & Mental Self Care

Spiritual Self Care

Social Self Care

Thoughts for the day

Tomorrow, I will...

_____
_____
_____
_____
_____
_____
_____
_____

Extra Self Care Challenge For the WEEK

- ☐ Spend some quiet time
- ☐ Take vitamins
- ☐ Get at least 7 hours of sleep
- ☐ Make a special meal
- ☐ Color or paint
- ☐ Plan a fun weekend
- ☐ Drink lots of water
- ☐ Set goals for the week
- ☐ Take time to reflect
- ☐ Get some fresh air

Daily Self Care Tracker

Date: _____

Physical Self Care

Emotional & Mental Self Care

Spiritual Self Care

Social Self Care

Thoughts for the day

Tomorrow, I will...

_____
_____
_____
_____
_____
_____
_____

Daily Self Care Tracker

Date: _____

Physical Self Care

Emotional & Mental Self Care

Spiritual Self Care

Social Self Care

Thoughts for the day

Tomorrow, I will...

_____
_____
_____
_____
_____
_____
_____

Daily Self Care Tracker

Date: _____

Physical Self Care

Emotional & Mental Self Care

Spiritual Self Care

Social Self Care

Thoughts for the day

Tomorrow, I will...

_____
_____
_____
_____
_____
_____
_____

Daily Self Care Tracker

Date: _____

Physical Self Care

Emotional & Mental Self Care

Spiritual Self Care

Social Self Care

Thoughts for the day

Tomorrow, I will...

_____
_____
_____
_____
_____
_____
_____

Daily Self Care Tracker

Date: _____

Physical Self Care

Emotional & Mental Self Care

Spiritual Self Care

Social Self Care

Thoughts for the day

Tomorrow, I will...

_____
_____
_____
_____
_____
_____
_____

Daily Self Care Tracker

Date: _____

Physical Self Care

Emotional & Mental Self Care

Spiritual Self Care

Social Self Care

Thoughts for the day

Tomorrow, I will...

_____
_____
_____
_____
_____
_____
_____

Daily Self Care Tracker

Date: _____

Physical Self Care

Emotional & Mental Self Care

Spiritual Self Care

Social Self Care

Thoughts for the day

Tomorrow, I will...

_____
_____
_____
_____
_____
_____
_____

Extra Self Care Challenge For the WEEK

- ❏ Hangout with friends for lunch
- ❏ Drink at least 8 glasses of water in a day
- ❏ Get rid of a bad habit
- ❏ Make-up your bed
- ❏ List fruits and vegetables to buy
- ❏ Follow a tutorial
- ❏ Play a game
- ❏ Watch a comedy
- ❏ Stretch for 5 minutes
- ❏ Go for a swim

Daily Self Care Tracker

Date: _____

Physical Self Care

Emotional & Mental Self Care

Spiritual Self Care

Social Self Care

Thoughts for the day

Tomorrow, I will...

_____
_____
_____
_____
_____
_____
_____
_____

Daily Self Care Tracker

Date: _____

Physical Self Care

Emotional & Mental Self Care

Spiritual Self Care

Social Self Care

Thoughts for the day

Tomorrow, I will...

_____
_____
_____
_____
_____
_____
_____
_____

Daily Self Care Tracker

Date: _____

Physical Self Care

Emotional & Mental Self Care

Spiritual Self Care

Social Self Care

Thoughts for the day

Tomorrow, I will...

_____
_____
_____
_____
_____
_____
_____

Daily Self Care Tracker   Date: _____

Physical Self Care

Emotional & Mental Self Care

Spiritual Self Care

Social Self Care

Thoughts for the day

Tomorrow, I will...

_____
_____
_____
_____
_____
_____
_____
_____

Daily Self Care Tracker

Date: _____

Physical Self Care

Emotional & Mental Self Care

Spiritual Self Care

Social Self Care

Thoughts for the day

Tomorrow, I will...

_____

_____

_____

_____

_____

_____

_____

Daily Self Care Tracker

Date: _____

Physical Self Care

Emotional & Mental Self Care

Spiritual Self Care

Social Self Care

Thoughts for the day

Tomorrow, I will...

_____
_____
_____
_____
_____
_____
_____

Daily Self Care Tracker

Date: _____

Physical Self Care

Emotional & Mental Self Care

Spiritual Self Care

Social Self Care

Thoughts for the day

Tomorrow, I will...

_____
_____
_____
_____
_____
_____
_____
_____

Extra Self Care Challenge For the WEEK

- ❏ Set 5 things you want to get done for the week
- ❏ Wear comfortable clothes
- ❏ Practice positive affirmations
- ❏ Cook a simple but delicious dinner
- ❏ Do something that makes you laugh
- ❏ Donate 3 items (books, food, clothes)
- ❏ Read something inspirational
- ❏ Let natural light in your house
- ❏ Moisturize your body

Daily Self Care Tracker

Date: _____

Physical Self Care

Emotional & Mental Self Care

Spiritual Self Care

Social Self Care

Thoughts for the day

Tomorrow, I will...

_____
_____
_____
_____
_____
_____
_____

Daily Self Care Tracker

Date: _____

Physical Self Care

Emotional & Mental Self Care

Spiritual Self Care

Social Self Care

Thoughts for the day

Tomorrow, I will...

_____
_____
_____
_____
_____
_____
_____

Daily Self Care Tracker

Date: _____

Physical Self Care

Emotional & Mental Self Care

Spiritual Self Care

Social Self Care

Thoughts for the day

Tomorrow, I will...

_____
_____
_____
_____
_____
_____
_____

Daily Self Care Tracker

Date: _____

Physical Self Care

Emotional & Mental Self Care

Spiritual Self Care

Social Self Care

Thoughts for the day

Tomorrow, I will...

_____
_____
_____
_____
_____
_____
_____
_____

Daily Self Care Tracker

Date: _____

Physical Self Care

Emotional & Mental Self Care

Spiritual Self Care

Social Self Care

Thoughts for the day

Tomorrow, I will...

_____
_____
_____
_____
_____
_____
_____
_____

Daily Self Care Tracker

Date: _____

Physical Self Care

Emotional & Mental Self Care

Spiritual Self Care

Social Self Care

Thoughts for the day

Tomorrow, I will...

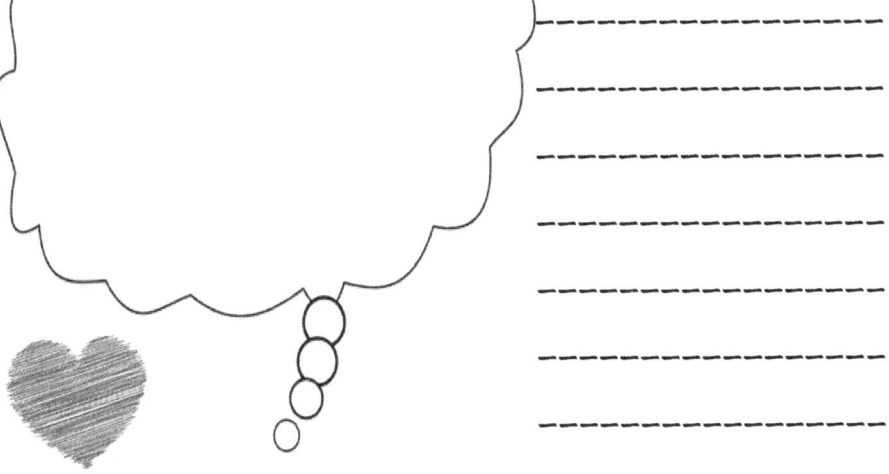

_____
_____
_____
_____
_____
_____
_____
_____

Daily Self Care Tracker

Date: _____

Physical Self Care

Emotional & Mental Self Care

Spiritual Self Care

Social Self Care

Thoughts for the day

Tomorrow, I will...

_____
_____
_____
_____
_____
_____
_____
_____

Extra Self Care Challenge For the WEEK

- [ ] Prepare an amazing breakfast
- [ ] Change your beddings and sheets
- [ ] Have a long steamy shower
- [ ] Take a 20-minute nap
- [ ] Replace 3 things at home
- [ ] Have a picnic on nice weather
- [ ] Eat ice cream or yogurt
- [ ] Thank someone
- [ ] Exercise for 30 minutes
- [ ] Practice mindfulness

Daily Self Care Tracker

Date: _____

Physical Self Care

Emotional & Mental Self Care

Spiritual Self Care

Social Self Care

Thoughts for the day

Tomorrow, I will...

_____
_____
_____
_____
_____
_____
_____

Daily Self Care Tracker

Date: _____

Physical Self Care

Emotional & Mental Self Care

Spiritual Self Care

Social Self Care

Thoughts for the day

Tomorrow, I will...

_____
_____
_____
_____
_____
_____
_____

Daily Self Care Tracker

Date: _____

Physical Self Care

Emotional & Mental Self Care

Spiritual Self Care

Social Self Care

Thoughts for the day

Tomorrow, I will...

_____
_____
_____
_____
_____
_____
_____
_____

Daily Self Care Tracker

Date: _____

Physical Self Care

Emotional & Mental Self Care

Spiritual Self Care

Social Self Care

Thoughts for the day

Tomorrow, I will...

_____
_____
_____
_____
_____
_____
_____
_____

Daily Self Care Tracker

Date: _____

Physical Self Care

Emotional & Mental Self Care

Spiritual Self Care

Social Self Care

Thoughts for the day

Tomorrow, I will...

_____
_____
_____
_____
_____
_____
_____
_____

Daily Self Care Tracker

Date: _____

Physical Self Care

Emotional & Mental Self Care

Spiritual Self Care

Social Self Care

Thoughts for the day

Tomorrow, I will...

_____
_____
_____
_____
_____
_____
_____
_____

Daily Self Care Tracker

Date: _____

Physical Self Care

Emotional & Mental Self Care

Spiritual Self Care

Social Self Care

Thoughts for the day

Tomorrow, I will...

_____
_____
_____
_____
_____
_____
_____

Made in the USA
Columbia, SC
06 May 2025